Funny Folks
in Limerick Land

Selected by
LELAND B. JACOBS
Drawings by
RAYMOND BURNS

GARRARD PUBLISHING COMPANY
CHAMPAIGN, ILLINOIS

A NOTE TO THE READER

This book includes "classic" limericks from such great writers as Edward Lear and Ogden Nash. In addition, it contains a large number of unsigned rhymes. No collection would be truly representative without the work of these "unknowns" who have done most of our limerick making.

The editor and publisher acknowledge with thanks permission received to reprint the limericks in this collection.

Acknowledgments and formal notices of copyright for all material under copyright appear on page 61 which is hereby made an extension of the copyright page.

Contents

Ouch!

A careless young lad down in Natchez
Burned his trousers from playing with matchez.
    To this careless young lad,
    "Bend down," said his dad.
On the seat of his pants he wears patchez.

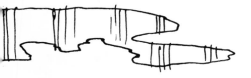

A Puzzling Problem

A puzzled young girl named Lorraine
Tried desperately hard to explain
    To a newly-met fella,
    "It's odd! My umbrella
Seems only to leak in the rain."

B. J. Lee

Wear and Tear

There was an old man of the Cape
Who made himself garments of crepe.
    When asked, "Do they tear?"
    He replied, "Here and there,
But they're perfectly splendid for shape."

Robert Louis Stevenson

Thin Sister

His sister named Lucy O'Finner
Grew constantly thinner and thinner,
   The reason was plain,
   She slept out in the rain,
And was never allowed any dinner.

Lewis Carroll

Expert

A prominent lady in Brooking
Was a recognized genius at cooking.
   She could bake thirty pies
   All quite the same size
And tell which was which without looking.

9

Fright

There was a young lady named Weems
Who, it seems, had horrible dreems.
    She would wake in the night,
    And, in a terrible fright,
Shake the rafters and beems with her screems.

Her Dream

On Saturday nights she goes backward to bed
And sleeps with her petticoat under her head.
    With a pretty pink bow
    Tied round her big toe,
She dreams of the prince she is going to wed.

At the Movies

I went to the movies. Alack!
I took a front seat in the back.
   I fell down—ah, me—
   To the first balcony,
And broke a front bone in my back.

A Slip

A housewife called out, with a frown,
When surprised by some callers from town,
    "In a minute or less
    I'll slip on a dress"—
But she slipped on a stair and came down.

Utmost Disorder

There was an old man on the Border
Who lived in the utmost disorder.
    He danced with the cat,
    And made tea in his hat,
Which vexed all the folks on the Border.

Edward Lear

Hostess

A hostess near Battersbee Landing
Had manners both bluff and commanding.
    It is one of her jests
      To trip up her guests,
For she hates to keep gentlemen standing.

Big Nose

There was an old man on a barge
Whose nose was exceedingly large;
  But in fishing at night
  It supported a light
Which helped that old man on the barge.

Edward Lear

Carrier

There was a Young Lady whose nose
Was so long that it reached to her toes;
    So she hired an old lady
    Whose conduct was steady
To carry that wonderful nose.

Edward Lear

Freddie's Reward

Freddie filled his father's hat
With nails and bolts and this and that.
    His father's belt
    He promptly felt—
Nor was it just a gentle pat!

Clean Rosie

A girl I know, Rosie De Fleet,
Is so very unusually neat
    She washes all day
    To keep microbes away,
And she even wears gloves when we eat.

Melancholy Lady

There was an old lady whose folly
Induced her to sit in a holly;
    Whereon by a thorn,
    Her dress being torn,
She quickly became melancholy.

Edward Lear

Startled

There was an old fellow from Cleathe
Who sat on his set of false teeth.
    Said he, with a start,
      "Oh, no! Bless my heart!
I've bitten myself underneath!"

Clumsy

A clumsy young laddie was Mulligan,
He recently acted quite dulligan.
    He climbed a wall,
    Then managed to fall
And landed *ker-plunk* on his skulligan.

J. B. Lee

All His Life

There was an old man, who when little
Fell casually into a kettle;
    But, growing too stout,
    He could never get out,
So he passed all his life in that kettle.

Edward Lear

The Young Fiddler

A chap who was learning to fiddle
Was good at "Hi Diddle Diddle."
    But with "Hickory Dock,"
    Though he played round the clock,
He always got stuck in the middle.

B. J. Lee

Stop!

A careless young driver, McKissen,
Just never would stop, look, and lissen.
    A train at great speed
    He gave not one heed.
Now lissen! McKissen is missen.

Lee Blair

Chin

There was a young lady whose chin
Resembled the point of a pin;
    So she had it made sharp,
    And purchased a harp,
And played several tunes with her chin.

Edward Lear

Frugal MacDougal

A bugler named Dougal MacDougal
Found ingenious ways to be frugal.
    He learned how to sneeze
    In various keys
Thus saving the price of a bugle.

Ogden Nash

A Thrifty Young Fellow

A thrifty young fellow named Shoreham
Made brown paper trousers and woreham.
 He looked nice and neat
 Till he stopped in the street
To pick up a pin—and he toreham.

An Old Miser

There was an old miser named Clarence
Who simonized both of his parents.
 "The initial expense,"
 He remarked, "is immense,
But I'll save it on wearance and tearance."

Ogden Nash

Caught

There was a young lady from Ayr
Tried to sneak out of church during prayer.
    But the squeak of her shoes
    Loudly broadcast the news
So she sat down again in despair.

Good Thinking

There was, in the village of Patton,
A chap who at church kept his hat on.
   "If I wake up," he said,
   "With my hat on my head,
I'll know that it hasn't been sat on."

Friz

There was once a small boy in Quebec
Stood buried in snow to his neck.
    When asked: "Are you friz?"
    He said: "Yes, I is,
But we don't call this cold in Quebec."

Sneeze

There once was a man with a sneeze,
Who always would sit in a breeze.
    When begged to take shelter
    He'd cry, "I should swelter!"
And straightway go on with his sneeze.

Mary Mapes Dodge

Neighborly

A chap came to town from North Bay.
He purchased a house right away.
   He said, "Neighbors all,
   My house may be small,
But I'm Cliff, so drop over some day."

B. J. Lee

How Come?

A hot-tempered fellow named Russell
Got into a fisty cuff tussle.
    When he heard people cry,
    "How come the black eye?"
He replied: "From a well-guided muscle."

B. J. Lee

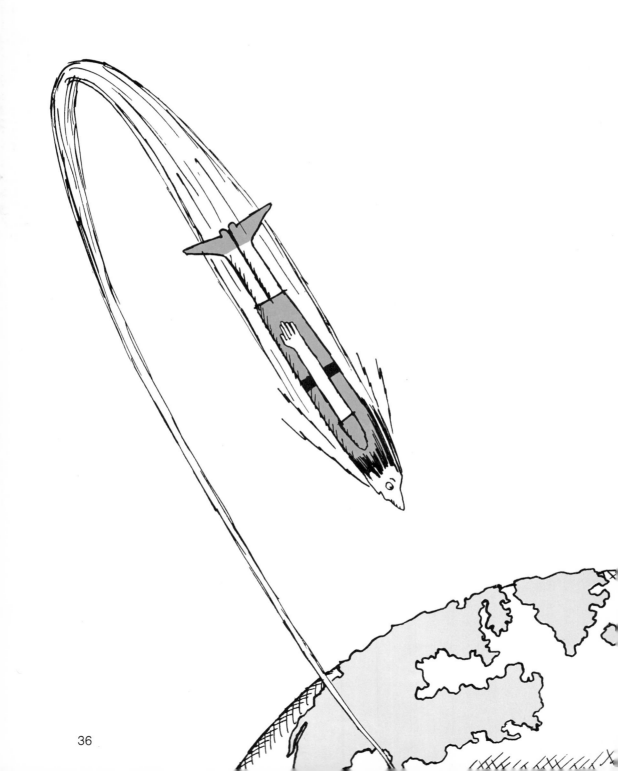

Unafraid

There was a young fellow named Greer
Who hadn't an atom of fear.
    He touched a live wire,
    As was his desire.
Most any last line will do here.

Too Wet

There was an old lady named Crockett
Who went to put a plug in a socket,
    But her hands were so wet
    She flew up like a jet
And came roaring back down like a rocket!

William Jay Smith

Sea! Sea!

A mermaid, as fair as could be,
Called out, "Please come swimming with me,"
    Which caused great commotion,
    And swells in the ocean,
As the sailors jumped into the sea.

The captain cried, "What shall I do?
On my ship this behavior is new,
    Yet I too have the notion
    To take to the ocean."
So he got in the swim with his crew.

Lee Blair

Joe McGoo

A funny clown named Joe McGoo
Brushes his teeth with pink shampoo.
    If you say, "Hi, Joe!"
    He won't say hello.
He'll blow pretty bubbles at you.

Pearl H. Watts

Don't Sing It

A young composer named Strong
Created a popular song
    Which he thought was great.
    But I hate to relate
It was bad even played on a gong.

The Winner

An astronaut speeding through space
With a witch on a broom had a race.
   The astronaut won.
   Said the witch, "I'm undone,"
And returned to the earth, in disgrace.

Elbee Jay

41

Tall

So tall was a cowboy called Slouch
He was taller than most in a crouch.
    When a horse stomped his toe,
    Pain had so far to go
Slouch three days later said, "Ouch!"

Seedy

There was a young farmer in Leeds
Who swallowed six packets of seeds.
    It soon came to pass
    He was covered with grass,
And he couldn't sit down for the weeds.

Ruined

A decrepit old gas man named Peter,
While hunting around for the meter,
    Touched a leak with his light;
    He rose out of sight,
And, as everyone who knows anything about
    poetry can tell you, he also
    ruined the meter.

$7 \times 1 = 7$
$7 \times 2 = 14$ $11 \times 1 =$
$7 \times 3 = 21$ $11 \times 2 =$
$7 \times 4 = 28$ $11 \times 3 =$
$7 \times 5 = 35$ $11 \times 4 =$
$11 \times 5 =$

More to Learn

A serious student named Lee
Could multiply seven by three,
 And all of the sevens,
 But of the elevens
He hadn't the slightest idee.

Before Six

When the teacher said, "Do tell me, Clive,
What comes before six, sakes alive,"
 Clive thought for a while,
 Then replied with a smile,
"What comes before six should be—
 the milk man!"

Lee Blair

Exam

"These test questions seem very clear,"
Thought a much-puzzled student named Weir.
　　"But I'm sure this exam
　　Will give me a slam,
For the trouble's the answers, I fear."

B. J. Lee

Spell It

You have to be brainy, not drippy,
To learn how to spell Mississippi.
    The i's and the s's
    Take knowing, not guesses.
(I think they are meant to be trippy.)

That's Loud

A teacher was trying to teach
His students the main parts of speech,
    But how he did burn
    At what they didn't learn,
So folks uptown and downtown,
    in alleys and highways,
    in buses and buildings,
    in all parts of speech
    heard him SCREECH!

B. J. Lee

Raisin Bread

Here is the reply made by Benny
When he was questioned by Lenny:
    "Do you like raisin bread?"
    "I don't know," Benny said,
" 'Cause I never have tried raisin' any."

Lee Blair

Very Absent-Minded

Absent-minded, in his shack,
An odd old man in Hackensack
   Was having supper rather late.
   He scratched the pancakes on his plate
And poured the syrup down his back.

Dinner Time

There was an old man from the Rhine
Who was asked at what hour he'd dine.
    He replied, "At eleven,
    At three, five, and seven,
And perhaps at a quarter to nine."

The Diner

There was an old person of Dean
Who dined on one pea and one bean;
    For he said, "More than that
    Would make me too fat,"
That cautious old person of Dean.

Edward Lear

An Apple a Day

"I must eat an apple," said Link,
As he gobbled one down in a wink,
   "For an apple a day
    Keeps the doctor away—
And I just broke his window, I think."

Lee Blair

Jammy

There was a young hopeful named Sam
Who loved diving into the jam.
    When his mother said, "Sammy,
    Don't make yourself jammy"
He said "You're too late, ma, I am!"

Elizabeth Ripley

More and More

There's a girl whom I heard of in Mich.
To know her I never would wich.,
    For she dines on ice cream
    Till with colic she'll scream,
Then orders another big dich.

Too Much

A greedy small lassie once said,
As she gobbled down slices of bread,
    "If I eat one more crust,
    I'm sure I will bust"—
At which point everyone fled.

Mighty Thin

There was a young lady from Lynn
Who was so exceedingly thin
    That when she essayed
    To drink lemonade,
She slipped through the straw and fell in.

Menu

They tell about old Dame Grundy,
Who always ate hash on Monday,
    And Tuesday too,
    And all the week through,
Except she had stew on Sunday.

Green Apple

There was a young lady of Ryde
Who ate a green apple and died.
    The apple fermented
    Inside the lamented
And made cider inside her inside.

Perfectly True

An old man from Kalamazoo
Once dreamt he was eating his shoe.
    He awoke in a fright
    In the dark of the night
And found it was perfectly true.

Acknowledgments

American Education Publications: For "Joe McGoo" by Pearl Watts. Special permission granted by SUMMER WEEKLY READER B, published by American Education Publications, © Xerox Corp., 1965.

Thomas Y. Crowell Company, Inc.: For "A decrepit old gas man named Peter" from *Laughing Limericks,* compiled by Sara and John E. Brewton. Copyright © 1965 by Sara and John E. Brewton. Thomas Y. Crowell Company, publishers.

Curtis Brown, Ltd.: For "Too Wet" by William Jay Smith. Reprinted by permission of Curtis Brown, Ltd. Copyright © 1969 by William Jay Smith.

Little, Brown and Company: For "Fragonard" ("An Old Miser") 5 lines and "Edouard" ("Frugal MacDougal") 5 lines from *Verses from 1929 On* by Ogden Nash, by permission of Little, Brown and Co. Copyright 1940, by Ogden Nash.

Henry Z. Walck, Inc.: For "Jammy" from *Nothing but Nonsense* by Elizabeth Ripley. Copyright 1943 Oxford University Press. Used by permission of Henry Z. Walck, Inc., publisher.

Index of Authors